Surprising Secrets
of Mystery Shoppers

10 Steps to Quality Service
That Keep Customers Coming Back

Surprising Secrets
of Mystery Shoppers

10 Steps to Quality Service
That Keep Customers Coming Back

by Anne M. Obarski

Printed in the United States of America.

ISBN: 1-932205-88-8
Library of Congress Control Number: 2003115588

Word Association Publishers
205 5th Avenue
Tarentum, PA 15084
www.wordassociation.com

Dedication

To my mother,
Helen Polasky

and my father,
the late Michael Polasky

Thank you for teaching me the importance of hard work, determination, and maintaining high standards in every area of my life.
I love you both!

Acknowledgements

The most gratifying part of completing this book is recognizing the hard work of all the people who have helped turn this dream into a reality. Thanks to all of you for your encouragement, your patience, and your input to help provide companies with a tool that will help them truly see themselves through their customers' eyes.

My Secret Shoppers: Thank you for your candid comments and great stories that gave life to what customers really wish management knew. Please continue to help make customer service a priority for every business.

My cover consultant, Sam Horn: Thank you for your wisdom, patience, and creativity in helping me to develop the title and cover design for my all-important, first book.

My artist, Jack Puglisi: Your talent and comical insight will make so many people smile through the wonderful cartoons in this book. I hope I didn't make you "stretch" too much! Believe me, it was all worth it! Thank you!

My editor, Lois Puglisi: Thank you for your professionalism in reviewing and editing this manuscript and for your constant support throughout this process. Your gentle spirit and wise decision not to let me see too many of the "red pen" corrections made this process painless! God bless you and Jack!

My Vice President of Marketing, Lynette Tomasetti: You are my cheerleader, my nudge, and my right arm! Thank you for all your hard work, from querying the shoppers to organizing the thoughts to finally getting it on paper! I am so proud to work with you and to call you my friend.

My super-supportive husband Jerry: Thank you for loving me when I get crazy, encouraging me when I lose faith in myself, and being willing to let me go as far as my dreams will take me.

My children, Meredith and Christopher: You are my pride and joy, and you both will have far better presentation skills than I will ever have. May you always touch and change lives with your God-given talents!

And a big "thank-you" to all my friends in the National Speakers Association, especially the Pittsburgh Chapter, for offering support, wisdom, information, and significant ways to shorten the cycle from just a dream to a reality!

Contents

Introduction

You might say that good customer service skills are in my blood. Though I didn't come from a family that ran a business, I was exposed to outstanding customer service while I was growing up.

My hometown is Cleveland, Ohio. I grew up in the mid-1950s in a modest home on the west side of town. Cleveland, like most big cities at that time, was proud of its diverse ethnic tapestry. My grandparents on both sides of the family came from Europe on the Lusitania in the early 1900s, so my parents are first-generation Americans. Categorizing people by their heritage was commonplace in our family.

My father described businesses by the owners' backgrounds. The local grocery store was owned by "a nice Italian family," the Rego's; the bakery down the street was run by a wonderful Hungarian woman; and the nursery where we bought our flowers had a Yugoslavian owner. "What kind of name is that?" my father would often ask when meeting someone for the first time. To my father, everyone's name had a connection to a country, and that country represented certain characteristics common to people who came from there.

The west side of Cleveland was made up of city blocks with well-maintained small brick homes that were encircled with wide cement sidewalks. As a child, I would regularly ride my bike to the grocery store to pick up a few items for my mom. I loved going to the grocery store all by myself! My mother would give me a list on a small piece of paper in her beautiful cursive handwriting. When I walked through the doors of the grocery store, I had a feeling of real independence.

Rego's was very small compared to today's large supercenters, but, as a child, I thought it was huge! The store was owned by four nice Italian brothers, as my father would say. The Rego brothers' "uniform" was a crisp white shirt, pressed black pants, and a clip-on, black bow tie. They all knew my mom, as she shopped there every week. She took me with her, and she would always dress me up when we went on our shopping trips. I remember that the owners would *always* say hello when we came in the store. They always made us feel *special*.

The store's bakery was a special treat. You could always smell the aroma of fresh bread when you came into the store. The ladies at the bakery wore starched white dresses that looked like nurses' uniforms, and their hair was pulled back tightly in hairnets to make sure it stayed neat. They were very serious about their work! I was always fascinated to watch one of the ladies behind the counter carefully use a special machine that perfectly sliced the warm bread. After it was sliced, she would remove it like a big brown puzzle piece and gently slide it into a crisp white bread bag without dropping a crumb.

The height of the wooden shelves on the angled bakery cases placed the wonderful goodies right at my eye level. My mother would always let me choose one item from the bakery, and I usually chose a small yellow cake with chocolate frosting that was rolled in the finest coconut. That is *still* my favorite kind of birthday cake! Again, the bakery ladies performed their jobs expertly. They would carefully place a piece of waxed paper in a white cardboard box and gently lay each pastry item inside. Then, from a large cone of bakery string, they would skillfully pull off the perfect amount of string to wrap the box so that it was secure. They would write the price on the top of the box with a black crayon and hand it to you as if it held the most precious jewels.

I remember that, as we walked up and down the aisles of the store, I would see the owners themselves actually stocking shelves. They worked efficiently, making sure that *every* can and *every* box was perfectly aligned. Yet, at the same time, they always noticed a customer and never missed the chance to smile and even call the person by name.

When we were finished with our shopping, a "carry-out boy" would stack the bags of groceries in a dolly-style cart, wheel them out to our car, and put them in the trunk for us! You didn't tip for this "service"; it was just part of what they did.

When their grocery business prospered, the brothers opened a number of other stores throughout the city. After I grew up and left Cleveland, my parents still continued to shop at Rego's and would inform me about births, deaths, and other important news involving the Rego family.

The Rego business was built on an "old world" standard: *relationships.* They made it their business to know their customers, what they wanted, and to satisfy them always. The lifeblood of their business was treating people like family. They were knowledgeable, efficient, and friendly. Most of all, they built *trust* in their customers' minds.

A number of years ago, the Rego family sold the business to a larger, out-of-state, grocery store chain. With this change came the slow loss of that wonderful sense of family and true customer service. New young families have replaced those of us who knew the "original" owners. Different standards for what constitutes good customer service have replaced those that defined our grandparents and great-grandparents entrepreneurship. As my mom says, "It's just not the same anymore."

Meanwhile, that little girl from the west side of Cleveland who used to ride her bike to the grocery store grew up, earned a Fashion Merchandising degree from Kent State University, and became a buyer in a junior sportswear department for the May Department Stores Company. I now had a hectic travel schedule that frequently found me in New York City, Los Angeles, and even Hong Kong.

I soon found that I had a different outlook from most of my fellow "executives." While they preferred not to deal directly with customers or employees, I loved working on the sales floor when I wasn't traveling. I was so proud when customers chose the merchandise I had so carefully purchased.

I learned on the job how important my customers were, and, even more importantly, how crucial it was to have great employees. I knew that my business was only as good as my best salespeople. They were the ones who looked my customers in the eye and took their hard-earned money so that these customers could take home items that I had bought with them in mind! I vowed never to act as if I was any better than those who worked for me. I helped at the register, bagging merchandise on busy days. The carnival atmosphere during big sales was invigorating! I opened freight, moved racks, ticketed, sold, hung merchandise, cleaned fitting rooms, and got to know my sales associates on a personal level. Those relationships were a two-way street and not ones I could have developed by sitting in my so-called "executive" office. My background and experience taught me what seemed to come naturally to the Rego brothers: *each individual customer is important* and *good service will make your business; bad service will break it.*

I learned that great customer service starts by developing great relationships with your employees. I trained a dozen assistant buyers who went on to become buyers in other areas of the store. I was truly lucky to have a number of experienced sales associates who proudly wore their service pins of ten, fifteen, and twenty-plus years of service. I knew them, their families, their favorite recipes, their birthdays, and their anniversaries. I had become a "Rego brother" in my commitment to my business and my staff.

Maybe that is why it was such a violent blow to my sense of business ethics when, during one of my yearly performance reviews, I was told by my supervisor that "if I didn't become more of an S.O.B., I would never make it in this business." To say the least, I was shocked at his attitude. My business had just hit the million-dollar mark, I had trained assistants who had been promoted to bigger departments, and my salespeople were some of the most talented associates in the store.

Now I was being told that I needed to be an S.O.B.?

"No way!" I thought. *"Sorry, but that is not how I built my business. That is not how I was raised."*

About a year later, I chose to leave the store that I had so loved. My life was taking a different direction that involved taking a leap of faith to start my own business. The business would combine some "old world" customer service ideas and some new corporate merchandising techniques to help business owners be more successful.

One of my first goals for my consulting practice was to help clients see themselves through their customers' eyes. Thus was born my "Secret Shopper" or "Retail Snoops" shopping service. I knew it was important to know everything you could about your customers before you tried to sell them your products or services. I saw how some companies had lost sight of that focus and were looking purely at their bottom line as a gauge of success or failure. So I hired people to shop in the stores of my clients and provide me with reports about their experiences: what the service was like, how they were treated, how knowledgeable the staff was, and so on.

Time after time, the Secret Shoppers' candid comments would help turn on the "lightbulb" in owners' minds, and we saw how making some minor changes could result in large increases in their businesses. The Shopper reports would frequently pinpoint areas of employee training that were lacking. Some employees didn't have answers to customers' questions, others didn't know how to do specific transactions on the register, and some displayed an "I could care less" attitude. The employees' lack of training frustrated not only the customers, but the employees, as well. By reviewing the "secret shops," we were able to uncover the clues that would help management better train their employees. We could also pinpoint what the customers wanted and then develop a strategy to satisfy that need.

Today, after almost two decades in the business, I thought it was time to share with larger numbers of current and prospective business owners some key things that customers wish management knew. The Secret Shopper stories are true, and we can learn much from them because customers everywhere probably have similar experiences with businesses every day. May we sharpen our focus as we look at both those whom we serve—and those who serve us!

Good, old-fashioned customer service comes down to you and me and the principles of the Golden Rule: treating others in the way that *we* would like to be treated.

Didn't your mom and dad teach you that? I'm glad mine—and their neighbors like the Rego's—did!

Chapter 1

The Litmus Test for Business Success

People like to do business with people they trust.

What does it take to make it—and keep making it—in business? Recently, a number of companies trusted by customers for many years have been closing their doors. Their customers lost faith in their ability to provide goods or services, or unethical scandals brought them down.

The true litmus test for business success is to gain and hold a buyer's trust.

Who would have thought that some of the big players in the retail world would be finding it hard to get new customers and keep their once-loyal ones? The reason for their decline is that many of them forgot a key element of their success: Every business has to work every day to focus on its most important asset—the customer.

I believe that the true litmus test for business success is to gain and hold a buyer's trust. In a study by the Booth-Harris Trust Monitor, 82 percent of consumers said "they have stopped using a company's products when trust is broken."*

What is one of the best ways to keep that trust? A business must be able to provide the goods and services it promises.

If you were to ask owners of retail stores why they decided to open up their own businesses, their answers would probably be something like these: "I saw a need for a product that no one else offered," or "I knew I could offer the product in a larger quantity,

---

*Source: <http://www.newswise.com/articles/2001/6/TRUST.BTH.htm> (02 April 2003)

in multiple sizes, with unique advertising, and with more creative displays, every day of the year."

Those are the original dreams of all entrepreneurs. They also used to be the dreams of some major discounters many years ago. Their inventory reflected what the customers needed in the appropriate sizes, quantities, and price. Yet recently I read an article in my local newspaper that helped explain what went wrong with those discounters. A woman in the article said the reason she changed her loyalty from Kmart to Target was that Kmart always seemed to be out of the items it advertised. She said she didn't want a rain check or a "blue light" special; she just wanted the advertised item. Is that request so complicated?

When I was a sportswear buyer at a large department store, a buyer could have been fired from the job if he or she ever ran an ad without having the merchandise in the store. There was never such a thing as running an "apology" in the newspaper stating that the advertised merchandise was not available. That statement might as well be followed by, "But you can find the item at our competitor's." If the customers want it badly enough, they will find out who has it, and they will go there to buy it. Supply and demand is the basis of good marketing!

How can you ensure that your supply will match your customers' demand?

Having the correct inventory is a matter of (1) managing your purchasing dollars to the customer demand, and (2) maintaining solid communication with the vendor so you can establish accurate delivery dates. Knowing the delivery dates of the merchandise you plan to advertise is critical for fulfilling your promise to your customers—and maintaining their trust.

The rules for balancing inventory are as follows:

Know *your* customers. Who are your customers? Where do they live, work, and play? What are the demographics of your typical customers? How long have they done business with you? What brings them back to your company? Do you just satisfy their needs? Do you address their wants, as well? There's an important difference between the two. For example, I *need* gasoline for my car, but I *want* to own a Porsche because of how I imagine it will make me feel when I am driving it. Offer your customers a selection of products that satisfy both needs *and* wants.

Know what *your* customers are willing to pay. Secret Shopper D. Smith of Puxico, Missouri, says, *"A company will gain a customer's trust by supplying a quality product or service at a fair price."* Your customers will tell you what price they are willing to pay. Poorly selected and priced merchandise is like old bananas. They don't get any better the longer they sit around. What old merchandise do you have "sitting around"?

Discover what vendors with whom you can build long-term relationships. The retail business is a relationship business. Relationships should be built not only with customers, but also with vendors. Each expects the same treatment from you: They want you to communicate with them frequently, always tell the truth, follow through on your promises, and show gratitude for their support.

Learn how to do both short-term and long-term predictions. Secret Shopper Helene from Vallejo, California, puts it simply: *"If you advertise it, have it in stock. If the stock moves faster than expected, encourage rain checks and make it easy for a customer to take advantage of this option. If rain checks are not an option, then be willing to substitute a comparably priced item."* Learn to test a new item to see if the customers are interested in it. Watch how fast it sells. Talk to your suppliers and find out who can provide you with reorders quickly. Acting and reacting, in record speed, is the name of the retail game.

Never be out of stock on "bread and butter" products. These products are the backbone of a business. They sell day after day

19

and are reordered and restocked like clockwork. This is not to say that there couldn't be fluctuations in their sell-through. Never make assumptions about basic stock items. Carefully monitor the turnover of your core inventory. After all, it is the heart of your business.

Know what your gross margin is so that you can frequently offer your customers their favorite items on "sale." Value is the name of the game. Offer customers what they want, when they want it, in the quantity they want, and at the price they want, and you will have satisfied consumers. But don't insult their intelligence. *"Don't call it a sale if it is not a sale. A $1.50 savings on a $35.00 item is not worth the trouble,"* says Secret Shopper Helene.

> *Offer customers what they want, when they want it, in the quantity they want, and at the price they want, and you will have satisfied customers.*

I taught retail marketing classes at the college level for fifteen years. One of the test questions I asked my students was, "List the 'Six Rights of Merchandising.'" Here is the answer:

> The Right Merchandise
> The Right Time
> The Right Quantity
> The Right Price
> The Right Location
> The Right Employees

Did you pass the test? Do you follow the "Six Rights"? Which ones do you have the most trouble with? Are you willing to do your homework to find out? Here's your "assignment": Study your consumers! Listen closely and take notes from your customers who trust you. After all, your customers have a lot to teach you!

Chapter 2

You Expect *Me* to Know What It Does?

People like to do business with people who are knowledgeable.

My husband loves toys. Not kids' toys, but what I call "big boy" toys. His favorite stores are Best Buy and Circuit City. He gets lost for hours playing in the video camera department: "Honey, look at this great, size-of-a-pea camera!" The smaller the better. I think he has a fantasy of living a life as a "secret agent." I can see him talking into watches and taking pictures with a camera disguised as a pen.

One day, we were shopping for the world's smallest video camera. Actually, this was the second time we had gone on such a quest. We misplaced the first one we had! My husband was thrilled that this new one was also a digital camera. What an upgrade!

The associate who waited on us at first seemed knowledgeable about the video camera and the type of printer we needed in order to print the digital pictures. He explained all the features and assured us that we would be able to print the pictures by using my laptop and the new color printer we were going to buy. But I should have known better when, after we made the purchase, he said, "This camera just came out, and I'm pretty sure it will work with this new printer and your current laptop." Hmmm. "Pretty sure," huh?

Six weeks and dozens of phone calls later to the Sharp camera company and the company who made my laptop, we were finally able to download all ninety-six pictures we had been storing. To do that, however, we had to make another visit to a different store to purchase a "digital media reader" that allowed my computer to see the pictures that were stored on a little disc the size of a postage stamp! The associate who helped us in that store knew exactly what he was talking about and had us out the door with the item we needed in less than ten minutes!

One of your most valuable assets is a knowledgeable staff.

No matter what kind of business you are in, one of your most valuable assets is a *knowledgeable* staff. Customers like to do business with people who know what they are talking about. How much knowledge employees have about products and services reflects the company's ability to train its staff initially and to provide ongoing training.

Quality training for all employees should be a priority for any business. Secret Shopper James of Portage, Wisconsin, says, *"There is nothing more frustrating for a shopper than to be passed along from one employee to the next because the employees don't have a complete understanding of their own products."*

Customers expect to deal with knowledgeable employees; they expect them to know what they are talking about. Here are three ways employees can gain the trust of the customer by demonstrating knowledge and experience:

Product Knowledge: Employees should have a working knowledge of the store's inventory. They should know what the products are used for, be able to explain the features and benefits to a customer, be ready to offer information regarding similar products, and, above all, know the pricing. That may sound simple, but Secret Shopper Natalie from Munhall, Pennsylvania, says, *"I cannot tell you how many times an employee has said the following to me when I asked about a product: 'I am not exactly* *sure what this product is used for, and I have no idea how much it costs.'"* What is even worse is *"when employees don't even know if they stock a particular item and are unwilling to do what it takes to find out,"* says Secret Shopper Leigh Ann from Conroe, Texas.

Common sense and efficiency is what customers will remember when it comes to having their problems solved.

Procedure Knowledge:
Employees should have basic store operations training. Generally, this is simple instruction on how to use a cash register, as well as how to handle returns, exchanges, charges, special orders, and so on. Customers expect that when an employee is behind a counter, he or she has been trained to handle any sales situation. Unfortunately, this is not always the case. It is important to train each associate for all the possibilities that could arise within a register transaction. When a customer makes a purchase, the cash-wrap area is the last place he or she will remember on the way out the store. Make it a pleasant and easy experience.

Practical Knowledge: Employees should be allowed to make commonsense decisions. For example, the Ritz-Carlton hotel chain teaches its employees to take ownership of a problem. They are encouraged to make a decision in the best interest of the customer and to do it as quickly as possible. It is always frustrating to be in a register line in which an associate has to page a manager to handle a question that probably has a simple answer. The associate more than likely knows the answer, but is calling the manager "just to make sure." Common sense and efficiency is what customers will remember when it comes to having their problems solved.

I believe customers create little "bank accounts" in their minds for every business they deal with. Each time they have a positive experience with a company, they deposit "positive experiences"

25

into that account. These deposits build the trust and confidence they have in a business. As a business's "bank account" increases, the customers are likely to recommend it to others based on all the good experiences they have had.

However, each time they have a negative experience, they make a huge withdrawal. Then they share those negative experiences with other people who have done business or could do business with that company. The negative stories they share usually center on an employee who lacked either product, procedure, or practical knowledge.

I want my customers to make positive deposits into their mental bank accounts for my business. I don't want to fill out withdrawal slips. Instead, I want them to refer potential customers to me based on the good experiences they have had. As the popular singer, Bonnie Raitt, says, "Let's give 'em somethin' to talk about!" Let's make that something *positive* to talk about.

Chapter 3

Why Am I Always in the Wrong Line?

People like to do business with people who are efficient.

There must be a talent to choosing the wrong checkout line in a store. I seem to be really good at it! Have you ever been in a situation similar to the following?

You are hurrying home from somewhere, and you are pressed for time, but you need to stop and pick up a few "essentials." You scope out the parking lot of the grocery store and dare the person coming down your aisle to take "your" parking space. Flying into the space, you jump out of the car, slam the car door shut, and avoid the look of disgust on the face of the person whose parking place you just stole.

In the store, you know exactly what you want, and you don't even need one of those cute little baskets to carry it in. You breeze through the aisles and round the corner to the checkout lanes when, suddenly, you stop short.

There they stand. Customers waiting ten people deep in each line, with only two lanes open. One of the lanes has its light flashing as the cashier waits for a price check. The other lane is manned by a brand-new employee who has to get an approval for a void from the manager. *Void,* in retail jargon, is just another nice word for *mistake.*

When this happens to me, various thoughts go through my head, like: *I could just leave these items on one of these shelves and walk right out the door. Who will notice the ice cream melting all over the candy and magazine aisle?* Better yet, I start looking for a manager who will try to take care of the situation by getting on the intercom and announcing, "All cashiers to the front lines." However, I have come to the conclusion that many cashiers have a lot in common with teenagers. They have marvelous selective hearing! This means that it would be a cold day in you-know-where before you'd see another cashier.

Every day, customers are weighing the importance you place on service and efficiency.

When I am held captive in a line, I find myself looking at my watch, sighing, or shuffling my feet so that the store employees will notice they are wasting my time. I even start to read the headlines on the tabloids. Usually, at this point, I also analyze all the "impulse items" at the checkout. The selection of merchandise that is on display is amazing! Phone cards, batteries, nail clippers, chocolate, VHS tapes, breath mints, and an assortment of old holiday candy no one wanted when it was fresh.

By the time it is my turn, I am tired and frustrated. The sales associate looks just as weary, and neither of us really cares about being sociable. My goal is to get my items checked and to get out as quickly as I can, hearing those cherubic words, "Have a nice day!"

We all have busy lives. We all get frustrated when we deal with businesses that waste our time. The X and Y generations have taught us to expect things quickly. They have discovered that you can watch a video in your van, go through a drive-through laundry, talk on your cell phone, and take bites of your fast-food dinner all at the same time, never missing a beat!

We definitely live in a hurry-up world. This means that running an effective business is even more critical than ever. Every day, customers are weighing the importance you place on service and efficiency. Here are four ways people decide whether or not you will get (or keep) their business:

Efficient handling of questions: Are your employees trained to be able to handle questions on their own and in a professional way? Do they get to the point, satisfy the customer, and represent the company in a positive light?

Efficient handling of the sale: Are your employees trained sufficiently before they are allowed to handle sales on their own? They should never have to tell a customer, "This is my first day, and I don't know how to do that."

Efficient handling of a problem: Do you allow your employees to role-play situations that will come up with customers? Do they know when they can make decisions on their own and when they need to call a manager? If they do call a manager, is there a chance the manager might override the sales associates' decisions—even though they are following store policy—thus making the employee look foolish?

Efficient handling of the job: Do your employees know *exactly* what is expected of them, every day, all the time? If the storeowner or president walked in unexpectedly, would you be proud of or disappointed in your employees' job skills? Do you have enough staffing, and does your staff have the tools and knowledge to offer customers an efficient shopping experience?

Sometimes businesses try to do too much and grow too quickly without having enough experienced employees. Bankruptcy is written all over these businesses.

Recently, I read that when the airlines cut back on flights after the 9/11 attack, ironically, a greater percentage of flights were on time, less luggage was lost, and customer service got better. The airlines improved their performance because they were able to focus on being more efficient.

It shouldn't take a wake-up call for businesses to become more efficient in serving their customers. Are you making it easy or hard for your customers to do business with you?

Chapter 4

Handle with Care!

People like to do business with people who are considerate and courteous.

Have you ever had your luggage "lost" by an airline? When you look closely at the faces of the people who are reporting their lost luggage in one of those little rooms at the airport, it is truly a sad sight. Their expressions reflect disgust, frustration, and even panic.

Actually, I have been lucky in my travels. The airlines have lost my luggage only once, and it was on a return trip. The airline delivered my suitcase to my house the next morning. But I do remember that horrible feeling in the pit of my stomach as I watched the almost-empty conveyor belt go around and around, with no sign of my luggage. I prayed that on its next trip around, my suitcase would magically appear through the vinyl flaps at the top of the belt. I wondered where my bag could possible be.

I once watched a television program where Erma Bombeck actually got into one of those plastic bins for suitcases at an airport and physically rode on the conveyor belt to see where our luggage goes from the time it is taken off the plane until we receive it! It was so funny to see her in that bin with her legs dangling over the side like a rag doll. "Hey Erma, you didn't see mine back there, did you?"

I realize that it is important to maintain some humor in such situations. Experts tell you to carefully label your luggage with a bright, unusual tag so that you can identify it quickly. So many bags look alike these days. You know, the typical black suitcase with a retractable handle and wheels—which people often carry on the plane to specifically *avoid* losing.

Businesses should treat each customer as precious cargo that they don't want to lose.

This process reminds me of a commercial I heard for an airline that says something like this: "Without proper handling, customers, like bags, are easily lost." That made me think! My plain black bag, as typical as it may be, is very important to me. What is inside it is unique, even special to me. I would be heartbroken if I lost that bag. Not because of the bag itself—that could be replaced. It's the items that would be hard to replace. And so it is with customers. Businesses should treat each customer as precious cargo that they don't want to lose.

Here are three tips to avoid losing customers:

Special Handling! Each customer is special. Your customers have taken time to call you or come into your place of business. They could have gone elsewhere, but they didn't. They deserve the best treatment you can give them. Put on the "kid gloves" and give them the preferential treatment they deserve.

Don't Assume! Often, business owners and their salespeople assume too much about their customers, such as: (1) the customer is just browsing, (2) she's not going to buy, (3) she's too picky, (4) she doesn't dress as if she could afford to shop here, (5) she's wasting my time, and so on. These attitudes can cause you to lose a sale. Never, ever, assume anything about your customers— except that they can shop somewhere else!

Courtesy Counts! Sam Walton once made a statement that went something like this: "The customer pays your salary, makes your vacation possible, and pays for your house and your car, but can dismiss you if you displease them." About 95 percent of customers leave a business because of inattentive, impolite employees. Can you afford to lose even one customer?

I recently ran across an article from a retail newsletter from the early 1970s that gave six hints about business courtesy. The advice is just as relevant today as it was then.

Hints about Courtesy

Be considerate of your customers' time by serving each in turn and as quickly as possible.

Extend a warm greeting when approaching customers and recognizing waiting ones.

Attempt to understand your customers' needs and help them arrive at solutions.

Listen closely to your customers' requests and politely answer their questions.

Be patient and pleasant with customers who are slow in making up their minds.

Show your appreciation for your customers' patronage by thanking them sincerely.*

Courtesy is a feeling best conveyed with sincerity and a smile!

The following experience of a Secret Shopper beautifully illustrates the value of courtesy:

My wife and I arrived at Ruth's Chris Steak House in New Orleans, Louisiana. We arrived at dusk and decided to use the valet parking, which was quick and very efficient. We were courteously greeted by a polished and professional "greeter" who immediately asked for our seating preference. We were enthusiastically guided to a beautifully appointed table that gave us a fabulous view of the city. We were attended by three separate waiters working in perfect concert. The food arrived promptly. The meal was well prepared, garnished expertly, and tasted beyond comparison. After-dinner drinks were mixed correctly so as not to intoxicate the guest. The bill

*O'Neilogram (1 November 1974) published by O'Neils Department Store, Akron, Ohio

was handled by the headwaiter in less than three minutes. Our vehicle was waiting for us as we exited the building. We are a military family and travel extensively. This restaurant gets our five-star rating.

If I am ever in New Orleans, I guarantee I will stop at that restaurant! Here's another excellent illustration of courtesy. The following excerpt is from an e-mail I received after I purchased an item from eBay on the Internet. I laughed so hard when I read it, and, honestly, when the item was delivered, I admit I sniffed the box to see if I could smell the lilac!

Your item was gently taken from our shelves of treasures and carefully placed into the best box in Roseville by a team of 30 packing experts. We lit a lilac-scented candle, and a hush fell over the crowd as we carefully placed your address label on the box. A parade ensued as the entire town of Roseville gathered together to march your package down Main Street to the post office, where we all hugged, cried and waved as your package flew out of the town on a supersonic jet to reach you as quickly as possible.

Such a clever idea intrigued me enough to go to their website to see what these "entrepreneurs" looked like! With just a simple e-mail, they had made me feel like a very special customer. That's because I'm a lot like that luggage on the conveyer belt we talked about earlier. I've been around the "carousel" a few times, and I know how it feels to be treated carelessly—as well as what it's like to be treated with special consideration and courtesy. So do your customers. Don't lose them just because you didn't realize how special they are to your business and its success. When it comes to customers, handle with care!

Chapter 5

Four Proven Ways to Recruit a Team of Excellent Employees

People like to do business with people who know how to hire good people.

I love watching kids play Little League baseball. It encompasses all the typical, delightful sights and sounds of summer: sunshine, warm breezes, hotdogs, and uniforms you never get completely clean! If you ever go to a Little League game, you'll see that the elements of the game are not very different from those of the major leagues. The players are smaller, but they emulate the "big league" teams. They have tough tryouts, practice daily, look the part, and support their teammates.

The key to recruiting quality employees is promoting and possessing a positive work environment, no matter how large or small your business is.

I think there is something special about the process Little Leaguers go through to learn to play organized baseball that can be transferred to the business world with great results. Independent retailers and businesses of all types, like Little League players, can profit by taking a few batting tips from the "big league" stores. This is especially true when it comes to choosing excellent team players from the field of new "draft picks" and "free agents."

I am often asked, "I am the owner of a small store. How do I compete with the big stores for great employees?" Here's my answer: Great employees are not *born*. They are *developed* in a business atmosphere where training is stressed, individuality is encouraged, and personalities are respected. Word travels about the work environment in stores of all sizes. The key to recruiting quality employees is promoting *and* possessing a positive work environment, no matter how large or small your business is.

Here are four proven ways to develop a strong team of employees:

Creatively Recruit

Focus on particular employment needs and develop job titles and detailed descriptions of the roles and responsibilities of each of these positions. These criteria will be beneficial in matching employees to specific positions. Later, in the review process, the same criteria can be used to measure employee accountability. They can also serve as the framework for advertising your available positions.

Would I want this person working for my competition?

Write several different help-wanted ads that can be positioned in various media. Be specific in your requirements. Ask yourself the following questions: What personality characteristics do I want, and what amount of experience am I looking for? Do I want "rookies" who will need a lot of training or seasoned veterans who will come with valuable experience? Then, go back to your list of criteria and decide on your "have to have" qualities, as well as those that would be "great to have," if possible. For example, if you need a candidate with a sales and managerial background, your ad might say something like this: "Seeking associate with strong sales record. Must have managerial experience."

Compete with large stores by attracting new employees through creative advertising. The ad must reflect the positive aspects of working for your company, such as "Specialty store seeking a highly motivated person to join our creative sales team. Fun

40

atmosphere and great benefits." One or more of the descriptive words must spark people's curiosity and make them want to respond to the ad. Try unique ways to advertise. Recently, I saw this sign in a jewelry store window: "If you like looking at our merchandise, you'd love selling it. Inquire inside." I had to hold myself back.

Hire and Interview with Purpose

Did you know that most people spend more time with the people they work with than with their own families? As you interview prospective employees, be conscious of personality traits that will be an asset or a possible hindrance to your team. Don't be afraid to ask

Training has to be an ongoing process to retain good employees and reduce the cost of losing employees in the future and of training new ones.

specific questions that the candidate *must* answer and take notes that you can refer to later. During the interview, ask questions that begin with phrases such as these: "Tell me about a specific time...." "Share some examples of...." "Tell me about how you handled...." Look for concrete examples, such as how an employee handled a difficult customer. If you ever find yourself wondering whether you should hire someone, ask yourself, "Would I want *this person* working for my *competition?*"

Power Train

Too often, small stores overlook this important component of developing a strong team of employees.

A recent study released by the Coca-Cola Retailing Research Council...put the annual cost of employee turnover in supermarkets at $5.8 billion dollars, an amount that exceeds that entire industry's profit by 41%! The study noted that these costs are from both training and hiring new

Employees are looking for a company where they can feel a sense of belonging and where it is recognized that their work efforts make a difference in the company's success.

associates, the damages and errors caused by inexperienced new employees and the "cost" of losing customers to a competitor due to the level of service being provided by the unskilled staff.[*]

High employee turnover can be costly to you. Training has to be an ongoing process to retain good employees and reduce the costs of losing employees in the future and of training new ones.

Your incentive should be to *train to retain.* Invite guest speakers, send your associates to seminars, and develop a library in a break room with motivational and sales training tapes that employees can borrow. There are a number of great video training products you can purchase for your employees. Team development should be an ongoing process, and a good manager should continually be looking for ways to add to this.

Reward, Reward, and Retain

Research has shown that money is not the number one motivational factor for employees.[**] Regardless of what type of work they do, employees are looking for a company where they can feel a sense of belonging and where it is recognized that their work efforts make a difference in the company's success. A good manager knows it is important to be a cheerleader as well as a coach.

---

*Andrea Waltz, "Paying Attention to Retail Retention!" Accelerating Retail Performance (May/June 2000): 1

**Source: <http://www.fed.org/onlinemag/dec95/motiv.htm)>(23April 2003)

You can reward all your team players by possessing winning characteristics yourself. Motivate your employees by allowing them to make suggestions, to take risks, to fail, to be challenged, and to succeed—all the while knowing that you have an open-door policy and will listen to their ideas and concerns. If the employees are happy in their jobs, if they feel appreciated, and if they respect the company's leadership, they will give outstanding customer service because they will enjoy what they are doing and the environment in which they are doing it.

Reward daily. Again, rewards do not always have to be monetary! A simple verbal compliment, a handwritten note of thanks, or a public acknowledgement at a weekly meeting are all nonmonetary ways of compensating employees. Review employee performance frequently, not always for the purpose of giving a raise, but to provide feedback on successes as well as in areas that need improvement. Finally, if you offer competitive salaries, benefit packages, and provide specific and achievable ways employees can advance within the company, you'll never have to worry about competing with the "big leagues" again. You'll hit a home run every time. Batter up!

BEWARE OF THE CLERK.

Chapter 6

Smile, It's a Customer!

People like to do business with people who are friendly.

Each time I work with a new client who requests a Secret Shopper program, I always begin by asking three questions:

"Why do you feel you'd like to have your business "secret shopped"?

"What information would you like to gain from this shop?"

"Would you share with me the 'non-negotiable' selling techniques your associates are required to use?"

The last question always seems to be the most challenging. The answer the client gives to this question automatically tells me something about the business's training program. Expectations for employees should encompass all aspects of customer service—from the moment customers walk into the store until the time they leave. If the client can answer very quickly what the day-to-day expectations for employees are, I know we are on our way to developing a successful program.

If a company is confident in its training process, it is easy to proceed. Yet, too often, store owners and managers *assume* their associates already know simple sales techniques, so

A "greeting" is much more than the words the associates say to the customers.

they never *teach* them. For example, you would think it would be easy to "test" how employees are greeting customers. However, most managers have never taken the time to spell out for their employees excellent ways to greet customers versus the types of greetings that turn customers off.

It takes your customers only about seven seconds to come to some crucial conclusions about the sales associates who greet them, including the following: Do they look professional? Do they act as if I am an interruption to their work? Do they seem to know what they are talking about? Do they appear trustworthy? The customers' first impression of your business is made in those first precious seconds. What would customers say about *your* associates?

A "greeting" is much more than the words the associates say to the customers. It is how the employees use all their communication skills with patrons. When I asked Secret Shoppers to share opinions on how they like to be treated and what they look for in an associate, they were quick to reply. Here are the top four skills that were mentioned by the Secret Shoppers:

1. Friendliness

A greeting must be "simply" genuine. I read an article recently in my local newspaper about a nationwide chain that is coming to my area. The article said that the company had interviewed seventeen hundred people for two hundred openings. Who were the successful candidates? Happy people who smiled a lot!

Isn't that interesting? The people who did best were not those who could sell ice to an Eskimo or who dressed in designer clothes, but people who genuinely *looked happy*. The article went on to say that this store wanted its employees to say hello to anyone who walked by and to ask customers who looked puzzled or uncertain if they needed help. The employees were also supposed to take customers right to the items they wanted, instead of just pointing out the correct aisle.

To me, that is genuine customer service. Tami, a Secret Shopper from Cincinnati, Ohio, says, *"I prefer being greeted when I enter a store. It shows that employees are interested in selling something to me. When no one says 'hello' to me or even asks if*

they can help me with something, I won't buy from that store."
Secret Shopper Laura from Wausau, Wisconsin, says, *"I would like to be acknowledged when I walk in a store and be said 'Hello' to. What turns me off is a fake 'Hello,' as if they are doing you a favor by saying it."*

My findings frequently show that about 95 percent of customers are not greeted when they enter a store. What is worse is that a customer may never be acknowledged the entire time he or she is in a store. How sad. A simple smile accompanied by direct eye contact is what most customers are looking for. Here are several more Secret Shopper comments about friendliness:

Mike from San Antonio, Texas: *"Just having a good and generally happy attitude can influence me and the amount, if at all, I purchase."*

Vickie from Monroe, Michigan: *"Employees don't have to have a smile permanently affixed in order to appear friendly, open, and approachable."*

Frank from Burlington, Vermont: *"A smile and a friendly face will disarm even the most discerning and apprehensive customer."*

2. Eye Contact

Many of my clients complain that their employees have trouble looking customers in the eye. I have found that this skill is difficult to "teach" to employees. Yet I believe it is one of the most important communications skills we can learn.

Linda from Kamloops, British Columbia, Canada, says, *"A friendly employee stops what they are doing to wait on you. They maintain eye contact, they smile, and they take a genuine interest in you as a person."* I also liked this comment from Betty in San Angelo, Texas: *"A friendly employee makes eye contact first, greets the customer with a smile, and makes the humdrum 'May*

47

I help you?' sound convincingly sincere."

3. Conversational Style

Unfortunately, there are certain employees who think that customers are interested in what they *don't* like about their jobs. This type of complaining is annoying to Secret Shopper Melissa from Comstock Park, Michigan, who says, *"I don't like it when all the employees do is talk about when they're getting out of work, when their break is, or how they don't like being there."* Associates should be encouraged to take the advice of Secret Shopper Maureen from Pasadena, California, who likes *"employees who greet you with enthusiasm that is sincere and not mechanical. They are courteous and make polite conversation so as to make the customer feel at home and welcome in their establishment."* Owners and managers must also realize the impact of their conversational styles on both employees and customers. I once witnessed a store manager reprimanding a sales associate in front of customers! That type of situation can make a customer turn around and walk right out of the store.

4. Body Language

Body language can say so much to another person. Avoiding eye contact, folding one's arms in front of oneself, and working on a project so intently as to avoid noticing the customer are all negative types of body language. Body language that *really* turns customers off is when employees are chatting with one another on the sales floor. Customers immediately feel as if they are interrupting an important conversation if they asked a question.

While doing a secret shop for a small store in the Midwest, I came out of the dressing room with a number of items I wished to purchase, but when I started to put them down on the checkout counter, the salesperson gave me the meanest look. "Do you think you could put them down *there?*" she demanded as she pointed to the end of the counter. "You'll mess up our card game." She wasn't kidding, either. The whole counter had playing cards spread out over it!

Pardon me, I just wanted to *buy* something!

Don't make it hard for customers to purchase your products and services! Smile—this is a paying customer!

Chapter 7

Bullfrogs Have It Easy—They Eat What Bugs Them!

People like to do business with people who understand them.

People enjoy doing business with people who are like them. People also enjoy working with people who are like them. Yet 60 percent of employees hate going to work every day.* Each year, one fourth of the workplace population receives treatment for mental illness or substance abuse.**
One of the main reasons is that many people have difficulty getting along with the different behavioral styles of their co-workers. As they say in kindergarten, these people have a hard time with "Works well and plays well with others"!

Either we can learn to get along with what "bugs" us, or we can be mean and *eat* what bugs us. Too many people choose the second option. Personally, I would like to live peacefully on the same lily pad with all the other bugs! We can do this by learning what motivates other people and how they communicate.

To help identify different behavioral styles, I have divided people into five unscientific categories, and I have named each of these categories after bugs. We all live in the same "swamp," and we see the same kinds of "bugs." Some people bug us more than others. See if you can recognize your customers, employees, and even yourself, in the following profiles. Then note some ways to communicate better and not let yourself be bugged by others.

---

* Source: Dave Jakielo (speech presented at the Laurel Highlands University Conference, Nemacolin Woodlands Resort, Farmington, PA, October 15, 2002)

**Source: Roxanne Emmerich. "Don't Look Now, but the Market for Speakers Has Changed," *Professional Speaker* 8, no 8 (March 2000).

Bee: Bees are driven. They are industrious and do well in management positions. Yet they also have short fuses. Don't bother them when they have had a bad day! Bees are abrupt, to the point, demanding, and may be considered rude by others. They leave short voice-mail messages, such as "Dave, it's Tim. Call me." (When they were in high school, they read the Cliff Notes rather than the actual book.) Bees are also are risk takers. They are the type of people who ride the highest and scariest roller coasters. They drive fast. They like the Black Diamond runs on the ski slopes. When they want to relieve stress, they usually choose something physical.

Communication Technique: Bees prefer a communication style that is clear, specific, and "bottom line." Suppose you work in the ticket sales booth at a Broadway theater. A "bee" person comes up to the window and says, "What are the three best seats you have? I need to know immediately, and I don't care how much they cost. Just make it quick."

Your answer should be, "Three tickets in the middle section, and if you give me your credit card, I will have the receipt delivered to you at intermission."

Fly: A Fly is an eternal optimist and everyone's friend. People like this are enthusiastic, expressive, talkative, and the life of the party. They like to socialize and become your friend. However, just like real flies, their continual "buzzing" can be annoying to others! For example, they may be hard to get away from at social gatherings. Flies like to write very long e-mails and forward cute pictures and tear-jerking poems they find on the Internet to a long list of friends and acquaintances. When you ask for their opinion, they love to share it with you. They hold positions on the PTA and are always involved in something. Spontaneity is their middle name. They are impulse buyers and like showy items that draw attention to themselves. They also live mainly in the moment, so planning or goal setting is not at the top of their priority lists. Flies do well in sales or in any position that involves a large amount of contact with people. When they are under stress, they probably pick up the phone to call someone or go shopping.

Communication Technique: Flies prefer a communication style in which they can engage others in conversation. If a "fly" person approached you in the Broadway ticket booth, the communication would be similar to this: "Hi! How are you? Great night for a show! Have you had a chance to see this show? I'll bet the costumes are just great, aren't they? Do you have three seats near the aisle, because I love to get out first for intermission to see who is here!"

Your answer could be, "Yes, here are your tickets right on the aisle toward the front. You will have a great view of the fantastic costumes, and your seats are in a perfect spot for seeing the romantic scene. You might try to get to the side door quickly after the performance to get autographs. Enjoy the show!"

Ladybug: Ladybugs are non-emotional. They are steady, reliable, and very patient. Good secretaries often seem to be Ladybugs. It's the mother Ladybug who can take ten children to the playground, only five of which are her own, and never have to raise her voice to keep order. Ladybugs don't drive very fast, and nothing ever seems to be a crisis to them. They tolerate conflict and never get upset about having to wait in a long line at the cash register. They like positive assurances, and you can count on them to be team players. If they were ever under stress, my bet is that they would just take a nap!

Communication Technique: Ladybugs prefer communication that is non-threatening and allows them time to think. If a "Ladybug" person were buying theater tickets, the communication might go something like this: "Hi. I hope I am not bothering you. Do you think you could check and see if you have three seats together, anywhere? Actually, I trust your judgment. You choose, and let me know how much I owe you."

Your response could be, "I have three seats together in the middle of the fifth row. I have sat in these same seats, and I know you will really enjoy the show from there."

Ant: The Ant avoids conflict and loves information! People like this are perfectionists. They are the ones who get straight A's in math and who love to read all the directions the night before Christmas on how to assemble the bicycle. They probably read *Consumer Reports* before they make any decision to buy something for the home. They always play by the rules—and coupons, calculators, and comparison shopping are rules they live by! Ants are often number crunchers. I am married to an Ant, and he is what I call a great "bean counter." If Ants are under stress, you just might find them happy to be alone, thinking!

> *Realize that people have different communication styles and needs.*

Communication Technique: The communication style of Ants is information-driven. They like conversation that is straightforward, and they need details to make a decision. If an "Ant" person wanted to buy theater tickets, the communication would be similar to this: "I have eight minutes to buy my tickets and get to my seat. Do you have three seats in the third row on the left side that are no more than $28.50 each? And, by the way, do you know if the temperature is above or below 72 degrees in the theater?"

Your response could be, "Yes, I happen to have those exact seats. As I ring up the tickets for you, I will call maintenance to check on your request, and I will have that information for you before you sign the receipt." (Okay, maybe this one is a little bit of a stretch, but you get the idea!)

The last bug comes as a suggestion from someone who recently attended one of my seminars. He came up to me and said, "Don't you think there are some people who are 'slugs'?" After a brief chuckle, I thought, *He's right!* so I came up with the following descriptors for the Slug.

Slug: The Slug just "exists." It takes a major crisis to motivate this type of person. Slugs are great couch potatoes. They don't have an opinion on anything. They could care less if they ate the same thing every day, wore the same clothes every day, and drove the same car their entire lifetime until they were buried in it! *Change* is the word they fear the most.

Communication Technique: This person would probably never go to the theater. After all, why waste the energy when you could watch a show on video from the comfort of your own saggy couch, with Cheetos and a beer? (Now we know why beer makes such good slug bait!) However, if a "slug" person were to buy tickets, the limited conversation would go something like this: "Just give me two tickets. I don't want to be here, but my wife dragged me out, and I plan to take a nap, anyway."

Your response could be, "You still have plenty of time to get to your seats. Here are two tickets about halfway down on the side aisle. They are near enough to the stage for your wife to enjoy the show, but far enough away from the action if you really want to take a nap!"

Did you recognize some "bugs" in your life? Have you come to realize that people have different communication styles and needs? This is why it can be difficult to teach greeting skills to sales associates. The worst thing you can do is to train associates to be a bunch of parrots. Instead, they need to understand personality types so they can communicate effectively with customers.

Suppose a customer walks into your store and hears your associates say the same greeting to everyone who walks in: "Hi. How are you today? If there is anything I can help you find, let me know." Next. That person will make the assumption that this is the extent of your customer service and that customers are treated in "cookie-cutter" fashion.

How do you avoid this situation? Teach your associates to be sales-and-service "spies." Suggest that they watch their customers' body language and eye contact and listen to their conversation styles so they can tailor the conversation to the customers' "bug" behavioral styles.

If customers are Bees, get to the point. If they are Flies, prepare for a long conversation. If they are Ladybugs, gain their trust. If they are Ants, know what you are talking about. And if they are Slugs, well, you just might have to do their thinking for them! Yet all your customers will benefit from the individualized attention—and so will you.

Chapter 8

If You Want to Leave a Message, Press 1

People like to do business with people who communicate effectively.

It's not what you say, but how you say it! This truth is especially applicable to the communication industry. What makes one TV newscaster more enjoyable to watch than others? Which radio talk show host is your favorite? Successful broadcasters know how to draw audiences to listen to them.

Branding is what successful companies do best.

Even though people's communication styles vary, there are some techniques we can use to help *us* be the ones our potential audience wants to listen to. Let's look at two types of electronic communication—voice mail and cell phones—and how to work with these technologies to communicate effectively with others.

VOICE MAIL MESSAGES

Most of us have at least one phone that is connected to an answering machine or voice mail service that has a message we want our callers to hear. Some messages are businesslike and some are funny. Some people like to use professionally produced prerecorded messages while others like to creatively produce their own messages that reflect their personalities.

If you are a business owner, your message should represent your company and its brand. Branding is what successful companies do best. For example, when I say *Intel,* you should automatically hear the four tones associated with Intel Pentium processors. If I say, *Aflac,* and you have seen that company's "duck," you might start mimicking the duck, saying, "A-flac! A-flac!" "You've got mail" is AOL, period. "We want to see you smile" is McDonald's.

What do your customers hear when they call you? If they get a voice mail message, how well does the message represent your company? Is it friendly, upbeat, to the point? Or does it sound as if the person who recorded the message was either forced into doing it or was bored with the task?

Do yourself a favor: Call your own company, listen to your recorded message, and ask yourself, "Does this sound like a company I would like to know more about? Does this message peak my interest and communicate professionalism?"

What about the voice mail messages *you* leave for *other* people? I find that, many times, it is not my first choice to leave a message for someone. I want to speak to a "live" person. I dislike it when a receptionist is clearly screening someone's calls and says, "They aren't in right now. Would you like their voice mail?" In these situations, I think to myself. *Now what do I say in less than a minute that will peak their desire to call me back?*

My husband hates leaving messages of any kind, for anyone. If he has to call the house, he leaves a message such as this: "Someone call me back, pleeeease." There's no "Hello," no "Hope you're having a good day," just a very impatient-sounding message. I realize I need to make a return phone call, but I will admit that in this situation I do so out of necessity, not desire. Everyone knows how to physically leave a message on an answering machine. The question is, do you know how to leave one in such a way that the other person will make it a priority to call you back?

Whether you are recording a voice mail message for your own business or leaving a message on someone else's voice mail, try to keep the following two techniques in mind to achieve the best results for you and your company.

1. Develop a thirty-second "commercial."

Develop your message as a thirty-second commercial for your business. Make it intriguing enough that the people calling will genuinely want to talk to someone and will leave a message. If the caller gets off the phone with a smile on his or her face or, better yet, *repeats* your message to someone else, that is a good thing!

A friend of mine who is a speaker has a very nice message that says, "As you can imagine, my business frequently takes me out of the office. I would like to talk with you about my seminars and consulting on the art of living well, so please leave me a message...."

You have learned two things from this message. First, she is a busy person working with many clients. Even if she isn't busy, it gives the impression that she is. Second, this person speaks about the "art of living well." I think I would call her back just to learn a few tips, wouldn't you?

What can you say in your message that will communicate to your clients and potential clients that you are the one they should be doing business with? Spend quality time perfecting your message and then practice it over and over before recording it so you can present it in a natural-sounding way.

The content of your message can also be the "commercial" you say when you attend networking functions or simply for those times when someone asks, "What do you do?"

2. Say it as if you mean it!

"I love you." Those are three simple words, but depending on the inflection you use, the listener can receive them in various ways.

Try emphasizing the word *I* first: *I* love you. That sentence makes you feel as though there is at least one person in the world who does! Next, emphasize the word *love*: I *love* you. Umm! That is romantic! Lastly, emphasize the word *you:* I love *you!* There's no question about *whom* you love.

All employees should be taught how to answer the phone properly.

I have heard people say "I love you" in a very monotone, non-expressive way. They have said those same three words for thirty years, and they think their family members should know by now that they love them. "If the feeling ever changes," they explain, "I'll let you know!" Yet inflection makes all the difference in showing sincerity!

How do you make your voice expressive? You practice the following vocal skills.

- Take a deep breath just *before* you start speaking, and begin to speak on the exhale. This gives you full lung capacity and a solid-sounding voice.

- As you practice your "commercial," decide which words need   emphasizing and where you should pause. Give "life" to your   words.

People make decisions about whether or not they want to do business with a company based on how someone answers the phone. All employees, no matter what level they are, should be taught how to answer the phone properly. There should be a unique and required way in which your company greets others by phone, and learning this greeting should be part of your employee training program.

Answering the phone is different from greeting a customer face-to-face. When you greet someone in person, you notice body language and eye contact, and you feel energy. When you answer the phone, the energy and excitement must be created. The way to create them is with voice inflection and a unique greeting.

First, consider the following: "Thank you for calling the ABC company. How may I direct your call?" This greeting is simple and straightforward, and it informs you that you dialed the correct number. However, there is nothing unique about it, nothing to make you say, "Wow!" If there is no inflection in the voice of the person who answers the phone, you may feel as if you are an interruption to the person's workday. Worse yet, you may think you have reached the evil "gatekeeper" who has no intention of helping you get to the correct person for fear you may "want" something of him or her—or of the company!

Now let's get creative. You can use a message such as this: "Good morning. This is Janice, your information resource at the ABC company. How can I make your call more efficient today?"

After developing a greeting such as the above, you need to choose where to make the inflections. Start with a deep breath and a smile on your face! "*Good* morning, this is Janice, your *information resource* at the ABC company. How can *I* make *your* call more *efficient* today?" When you create a unique greeting with specific inflections, the caller will sense the energy and feel well taken care of because of the friendliness and efficiency of the person answering the phone.

To finish the process, let's assume Janice has to forward the call. Janice can win the caller over by saying, "It would be a pleasure to transfer you!"

Is the communication process over at this point? No! The next person who answers the phone should demonstrate the same positive communication skills that were established by the person who initially answered the call. As Mom always said, "First impressions count!"

CELL PHONES

I am often slow to embrace technology! It takes me a while to learn how to handle new gadgets and use them with any regularity. It took me some time before I became best friends with my microwave, and I am still a little clumsy when using our video camera. My Palm Pilot is a backup to my desk calendar, instead of the other way around. And I made a New Year's resolution with my almost-sixteen-year-old son that I would keep my cell phone on when I am away from home. That has been the toughest resolution for me to keep (along with remembering my cell phone number!).

I must admit that I still don't like cell phones. Companies keep making them smaller, and they just don't fit my face. There are times when I feel that I can't talk and listen at the same time because the phone doesn't reach from my lips to my ears! Then there is the itty-bitty keypad. No wonder people get into car accidents while they are trying to dial! What is even more challenging is trying to dial a cell phone in the car *at night*. With my manicured nails, it's a wonder I haven't dialed Zambia by mistake!

There is a part of me that becomes jealous when I watch other people use cell phones. First, I get the impression that these people are so popular that others can't wait to talk to them. Then, I imagine that all those phone calls they receive are instant business deals because the other person can't wait until he or she gets to the office to seal the deal. I know a woman who would wear a phone headset when boarding a plane—the kind with the mouthpiece that curls in front of your mouth—and just keep talking on the phone as she walked down the aisle to her seat. I always wondered who she had to talk to so badly.

Then there are people who use cell phones while shopping. These customers are definitely "multi-tasking"! They can carry on a phone conversation while walking from store to store, trying on clothes, and (probably) paying for them—without missing a beat. Yet if you're a store employee, how do you interact with a customer who walks into your store already glued to his or her "cell"? What kind of greeting can you give?

Here are some pointers for dealing with customers who are constantly on their cell phones.

1. Don't try to compete with their conversations. You are secondary in importance to them, and it will only confuse them if you try to ask them a question.

2. Try to make eye contact. This will be tough because they are already mentally preoccupied. However, as you are walking past them, you can smile and give them a little wave. In this way, you are helping them come back to reality. After all, they *have* walked into your business for a reason.

3. Remind them that they are in a place of business. Have you ever noticed how loud some people are when they use cell phones? In a store, this is annoying for other customers as well as for the employees. No one wants to listen to someone else's phone conversation. To encourage them to hang up, without saying such, try to be physically working wherever they happen to be standing or browsing. You can move inventory, fold clothes, check fitting rooms, talk to other customers, or do anything else to let them know they are in a place of business. You can even ask other employees questions right in the same vicinity. When the people feel as though they are competing with their surroundings, they will probably opt for ending their calls.

I believe cell phones have a place. They have become a necessary part of our daily lives. However, I also believe that some people lack common courtesy. How many times have you found yourself in a checkout line where the employee is on a personal call or having a conversation with another employee and totally ignoring you? (People don't need a piece of phone equipment to be unaware of what is going on around them and what they should be doing. It's not the cell phones themselves that are bad, but the ways in which people use them.) Recently, during my speaking engagements, people in the audience have been receiving calls on their cell phones. When this happens, all eyes and ears become focused on the person with the phone call, not where I want the attention to be. Sometimes I will say to the whole group, "I told them not to call me at work!" That humorous but pointed comment usually makes the person receiving the call *end* it very quickly!

We need to remember to BE in the present when communicating with customers.

Building relationships with clients is a give-and-take process, and good communication is also give-and-take. When one party is preoccupied, it becomes much more difficult to nurture the relationship. Sometimes we don't realize we have tuned the other person out. We need to remember to *be* in the present when communicating with customers.

New technologies are changing the way we live and how we do business. This will continue to be the case in the future. Adapting good communication strategies to these new technologies will enable us to stay current with our customers and be the ones who gain and keep their attention!

Chapter 9

Retail Business Is Show Business!

People like to do business in a pleasant, unique atmosphere.

I never realized how much "theater" there is in retailing! I was in a management meeting the other day, and one of the store managers said that when he is working with a customer, he makes sure he never has his back to the front of the store so as not to miss a customer coming through the door. He went on to say that this technique enables him to keep watch over the whole store when scheduling is tight. It also helps him to be more observant of possible shoplifters.

He was so right! Whether he realized it or not, that manager was using a basic theatrical "staging" technique. Whenever an actor is on stage, his or her body should be facing the audience as much as possible at all times. In the same way, your "audience"—your customers—need to hear you and have eye contact with you, for this is where true communication begins.

Keeping communication lines open with customers is especially important in today's marketplace because retail salespeople are turning into "task" employees. With payroll being trimmed right and left, employees are expected to do more than wait on customers. They are expected to "run the show." If this is the future of retailing, then here are some additional tips to help you "break-a-leg"!

The Actors

I think the hardest job for any director must be casting. Directors have to deal with people's egos, personalities, and demands. Yet so does any good store manager or human resource director. With the pool of qualified employees dwindling, it is important to do the best you can when you hire, and to *train, train, train.*

I am finding that, more and more, companies are abandoning their training departments.
They are putting that responsibility on either the store manager or the regional manager. Many times, training just doesn't get done, so it turns into OTJT (on the job training). Yet who trains the manager? You can't be in a play unless you know the script. It should be the same in any business. All employees should know the following:

- **The company mission and vision statements. In other words, what do you stand for?**

- **All company procedures and policies.**

- **The company "non-negotiables." These are the things that every employee should be able to do, such as specific ways to greet the customer, answer the phone, transfer calls, or handle complaints. Employees should know when to call for a manager and when they can make their own decisions or do "improv."**

- **Whatever they are trained to do, they should be able to be tested on and be held accountable for.**

I don't know one person who goes to the theater and doesn't come out saying to someone else, "Did you like it?" Most of the time, that question refers to what the person thought about the performance of the actors. Were they able to draw the audience in, develop a relationship with them, and make them feel as if they truly knew them by the end of the play?

Sometimes actors change roles as the play progresses. That is also what good retail employees can do. Again, in most businesses, the days of having a large staff seem to be gone. Employees often need to greet customers while doing other tasks. They follow up while they are walking past the customers on their way to perform other duties. They polish mirrors, fold clothes, check fitting rooms, put out inventory, train new associates, and, yes, ring up sales. Do you know what the performance of your employees is like? Can you evaluate it?

All in all, the question is this: Do your employees make their "audience" feel special? The challenge of multi-tasking is not letting the customer feel like an interruption to the employee's day. That is why it is so important for associates never to turn their backs on a customer, no matter how busy they are. The audience is watching!

The challenge of multi-tasking is not letting the customer feel like an interruption to the employee's day.

The Script

I have always wondered how actors can do the same play night after night and still make it look as if it is opening night! Inside, I know they must be tired of saying the same lines, over and over again. But I'll bet that if you were to talk to an actor, he or she would say that it is not the lines but the *audience* that makes the performance fresh every time. I would also imagine that if an actor could see the people in the audience distinctly and recognize repeat attendees, that would be an added encouragement!

So it is with people in any sales position. The first day on the job is exciting! But each day has to be like "opening night," even when you just don't feel like it. The following story shows the difference between a rote performance and a fresh one.

The other day I walked into a golf shop to look for a pair of shorts. I was "greeted" by a man standing next to the cash wrap with his arms folded in front of him, looking just like a statue. He said, "Hi, how are you?" with about as much excitement as someone who has just had a root canal.

I walked all around the store, picked out a pair of shorts, tried them on, and came back to the wrap desk. He never moved. It was amazing! He looked like a store prop. Luckily, a gal from the ladies area came to suggest a top to go with the shorts I was buying. She then said, "Did you get a chance to see the new fall group we got in? Well, you just *have* to see it!" I followed her all around the clothing section like a puppy.

The other associate stayed planted in that one spot as other customers came and went. The gal I was working with recognized a male customer and caught his attention as he was walking out the door. "Tell your wife we have two new Tehama groups that just came in," she said with a big smile. "Thanks for letting me know," he said. "I'll send her in!"

Annette, the friendly sales associate, didn't have a rote script or canned questions to ask customers. She was able to build relationships and carry on conversations that made you want to spend time and, eventually, money with her. She also did something else. Through her sincere personality, she built trust.

I didn't spend very much money that day, but you can bet I'll be back in her "audience" many more times, and I'll be sure to tell everyone I know, "You have to go see Annette!"

I'm sure you've had similar experiences. You've seen sales associates who were merely going through staged motions, ready for the day to be over, as well as true "actors" who love their jobs and want to perform at their best, every day, in front of every audience.

The Stage

There is something about going to a Broadway show that is mesmerizing! The props, the costumes, the orchestra, and the set design all create the excitement that you go to the theater for. Retail stores are not much different. The fixtures, flooring, lighting, and layout all contribute to the ambiance of the store. Customers expect that. What's more, merchandising has really gone high tech! For example, it is not unusual to see Old Navy employees wearing communications headsets so they can quickly respond to a customer's needs.

When was the last time you looked at your store as a stage? How is the lighting? Is it old and inadequate? What about the fixtures? Do they *feature* merchandise, or have they become another place to "house" merchandise? Is there music playing in the store or is there dead silence? Have you really looked at who your customers are and then decided what music you would like to have playing in your store to attract them?

Pretend you are going to your store as you would go to the theater. Look at everything from the glass on the front door to the smell of the store to the staging within the store. Secret Shopper Mary from Bethel Park, Pennsylvania, shares, *"When I walk up to a store that has fingerprints all over the door and a dirty entrance, I automatically make the assumption that the whole store is that way."* Meredith from McMurray, Pennsylvania, said, *"When I go into a fitting room that has dirty carpet and there are hangers, tags, and clothing left by someone else, that is the biggest turn-off for me to want to spend money in that store."*

The Show

I must say I was a skeptic when Target first came to our city. What is it that makes Target so appealing and popular with customers? I discovered that it isn't just one thing. It is the whole show!

Branding

I believe it all started with the red Target logo. It is simple and memorable. In fact, it is so memorable that they now can make it any color they want, and most people know exactly whose advertising it is. What does your "brand" look like? Is it easily recognizable? Do you use it on everything that your customer comes in contact with?

Merchandising

Target stores look great all year round. They never make excuses that they are out of stock or were short-shipped

73

or lack the manpower to make the store look great. The merchandising is artistically done. It is never overpowering. It is clean, neat, and customer friendly. The front entry of the store is always seasonally centered. Maybe it is the abundance of red color in the store that makes me feel excited when I walk in the door. Whatever the methodology, it is fabulous.

Extras

Target makes it easy to shop at its stores. The business is well thought out and orchestrated. Plus, Target reaches out to markets that many stores have avoided. One is the wedding market, and another is the baby market. As I have said before, the litmus test of any good business is to gain and hold a customer's trust. If new generations shop at Target as children, then register for their wedding and baby shower gifts as adults, do you think they will trust Target? You bet they will–and do!

Target is a great "show"! Customers go back to see what is new "on stage." They like Target's "actors" and coming attractions. Who are *your* actors? Are their scripts rote memorization or customer-oriented? What does your stage look like? What does your whole show say about you?

If you put thought, creativity, and effort into "producing" your business, every night will be like opening night. Curtain's going up. It's show time!

Chapter 10

Are Your Customers Worth It?

People like to do business with people who don't take them for granted.

Years ago, there was a hair-color commercial on TV that had a memorable line: "I'm worth it!" The company used different actresses over the years, but each one repeated those words. The saying was transferred to the popular culture and was used by people in various situations to emphasize the fact that we *are* worth it. Worth what?

Worth being treated by the Golden Rule: "Do unto others as you would have them do unto you"—period. I know there are other "rules" that are spin-offs of this one, but I like the old one best. For business owners, this rule represents a kind of insurance policy.

Insurance bills are something I hate to pay, but they are necessary. I don't seem to have anything tangible after I pay them, and I may never have to use the insurance. However, it would be just my luck if I let the bill slide for a month. Something terrible would happen, and I would need that insurance in a hurry.

I have insurance because "I'm worth it"—worth protecting. I am a wife, a mother, and a business owner. I have worked hard, and I think I deserve the "comfort zone" that insurance brings me. One of the insurance plans I have is emergency road service with the American Automobile Association, better known as AAA. I haven't had to use it very often, but it is nice to know that, if anything should happen, help is only a phone call away. I live in Pennsylvania, and winters here can be treacherous. We never know when we could get stuck in a terrible snowstorm.

On one occasion, however, I needed to be towed in late spring. I had gone to my son's baseball practice, and I had driven my car up to the field and parked on the road in a line with all the other parents. To make room so that others could pass us, we had all pulled over to the right-hand side of the road so that the tires on the passenger sides of our cars were off the road in the dirt. It was a very wet spring, and the area that my car was in had just been seeded. I hadn't noticed that when I got out of the car. Two hours later, I returned to find my passenger side tires submerged in the mud and my car tilted at what looked like a forty-five-degree angle. Worse yet, mine was the *only* car that looked that way!

Every day, our employees have the opportunity to show customers that they are worth our time and attention.

I can't tell you how many "comments" I got from other parents who walked past my car! Luckily, when I called the number on my AAA card, they didn't laugh. They sent someone out quickly. How busy could AAA be on a sunny May afternoon? The tow truck driver was polite (though he probably snickered when I couldn't see him) and pulled my car safely out of the oozing mud. My insurance was worth it that day. Insurance is always worth it. It is worth it because we are worth it. It is a comfort zone!

Similarly, our businesses should offer a comfort zone for our customers. This "insurance" for the success of our companies can't be purchased, but it can be developed. Every day, our employees have the opportunity to show customers that they are worth our time and attention. We have touched on the following three areas in other chapters, but they are ones you must especially focus on to maintain a "AAA" rating for your company.

Attitude
Sometimes customers receive the "I have had a bad day" attitude from employees. Three out of four customers leave a store because of impolite, inattentive salespeople.* The customer

doesn't deserve that treatment. As we talked about in chapter nine, your store is like a stage, and the employees are the actors. Every day is "opening night," and you want to receive good "reviews" so that you can have a long-running show. Have your employees leave their problems outside the store and polish their performance. It's time to *wow* the audience.

Attitude, awareness, and audience—are the basis of good employee training.

Awareness

Always be aware of what is going on around you. Sometimes sales associates feel that they are in an isolated bubble behind the service desk and never have to move or approach a customer. That may have been true years ago, but not now. Employees have to perform many tasks *and* take care of customers. The old saying, "You need eyes in the back of your head," has never been truer. Encourage your employees to be alert. Your customers are watching!

Audience

Actors can tell whether or not they have the audience's attention: All eyes are on them, and the audience is riveted to every word. Nothing else that is happening is more important than the relationship between the actor and the audience. This relationship is actually no different from the relationship between the sales associate and the customer. Greeting the customers, making eye contact, listening to their needs, and finding a way to satisfy their wants are all part of being a good associate.

These three words—*attitude, awareness,* and *audience*—are the basis of good employee training. Have a positive attitude; always be aware of your customers, whether they are in your store or on the phone; and, most importantly, be sensitive to your customers'

---

*Approximate figure based on Merchandise Concepts' Secret Shopper evaluations conducted since 1988.

needs. This is your business insurance. You can bank on it!

The following story teaches some important lessons about how you can let your customers know that you think they are worth being treated and served well. I am sure we have all had a "pink jacket" at some point in our lives!

What one outfit do you own that, when you put it on, you say, "I look good"? It might be the outfit that got you the job on the first interview. It might be what you wore when you made a dynamite presentation. Maybe it is what you wore when you proposed.

Whatever the outfit, it is important to you. I have a pale-pink silk jacket that I just love. I had my picture taken in it for my business cards, and I have worn it frequently to do presentations when a bright color might be too strong. When I put that jacket on, I feel wonderful. I pray that it doesn't go out of style for a few more years because I would really miss wearing it!

But sometimes terrible things happen to the things we love best. So it was with my pink jacket. I was using a blue pen, and I brushed blue ink on the front of the jacket. I thought to myself, *Doesn't hairspray take out ink spots? Sure it does. No need to take this to the cleaners for such a small spot.* I carefully sprayed some hairspray on a cloth and rubbed gently on the spot. Well, you guessed it. That *small* spot grew. Now it was a bigger wet spot with a large blue spot smack in the center of it. I had the worst feeling in the pit of my stomach. Why hadn't I just taken it to the dry cleaners? They can do magic!

Even though I was embarrassed to tell the dry cleaners what I had done, I didn't have a choice about it because I was *not* getting rid of my jacket, and I couldn't wear it the way it was. I took it to the dry cleaning store that I had been dealing with for at least fourteen years. This store is very plain and, like most cleaners, is located in a strip mall. When you come through the front door, there is a small area with a couple of white plastic patio chairs and a fixture of men's ties that is never filled. (I always wondered why a dry cleaning store would sell ties, anyway!) Music is usually playing loudly from an old "boom box," and the door is always propped open, as they have no air conditioning.

The ownership has changed hands only once, and the woman who works behind the counter has been there since the beginning. She is very quiet and never makes any eye contact; she processes items without ever taking a good look at what is brought in. I've often thought I could bring in a dead cat with my husband's shirts, and she would probably tie them up together and throw them in the pile with the rest of the "light starch, on hangers" group.

When I walked in that day, I carefully laid my jacket on the counter and was prepared to be questioned about what *I* had done to the jacket. I was even ready to take some well-deserved scolding. Instead, she never looked up. She just asked, "Name?" Stop right there. Name? I have been bringing in laundry weekly for fourteen years. Over that time, I have probably given the store about $8400 worth of business, and she doesn't know my name? Then she said, "Phone number?" Okay, I figured that if she didn't remember my name, she surely didn't remember my phone number. She continued to fill out the pressure-sensitive slips without looking up. I quietly mentioned that the jacket had a stain that needed to be taken out. She quickly flipped the jacket around and said, "Did you try to do something to this stain?" At that moment, I felt just like a five-year-old who has to tell her mom what a mess she has just made. I related the story, and she just rolled her eyes, pulled out a yellow sticker, slapped it on the jacket, and tossed it into the pile. My heart sank. To her, my beautiful pink jacket was just another hassle to be dealt with.

Then she handed me the infamous "pink slip" and told me it would be done in a week. I prayed that they could get the stain out, but she never indicated one way or another. I made sure I picked up my jacket that next week. When I went in, I was greeted the same way as usual. I didn't check my jacket, but I was sure they had done their magic before placing it in that clean plastic bag, ready for me to be "superwoman" in it once again.

When I got home, I checked the jacket, and attached to it was one of those nasty little tags that says, "Sorry. We tried to get the stain out, and this is the best we could do." Sorry? You have to be kidding. I checked out the stain. The ink was gone, but the ring was about three inches wide. When I put the jacket on, that ring looked like a flashing beacon to me. I thought, *Well, maybe I can wear the jacket when I go grocery shopping, because I surely can't wear it to do business presentations.* My poor jacket hung in my closet for months. I knew I would never find that color again, and I told myself it was a lesson learned. (I frequently do that when I mess up!)

A few months later, I had to drop off my son's band uniform at a different dry cleaning store. The high school had chosen this cleaners because it did excellent work. I had never used this store because I had heard its prices were "too expensive." While I was there, I remembered my pink jacket just hanging in my closet, and I asked if they would take a look at it if I brought it in. The woman I talked to was wonderful. She told me about their establishment and about the man who does all their dry cleaning. She said he has been in the business for thirty years, and she knew he could fix my jacket. I took her up on her offer and brought my jacket in, still in the plastic bag. She looked at it and said, "I don't think this will be a problem at all."

When I left the store, I was walking on air. I trusted what she said, and I knew why they charged a little more than the other area cleaners did. They had someone who *cared* about my clothes— and me! When I went back to get my jacket, I was anxious to see if the man had performed the magic she had promised. She took the jacket out of the bag for me to inspect it.

You guessed it. There wasn't a hint of a spot or mark on that beautiful silk jacket. Pro Cleaners in McMurray, Pennsylvania, knew how to clean my superwoman outfit. They have won my trust and my business for my special clothes. The photo of me in my pink jacket is now on my website. Don't you think that is

Focus on ways to retain and multiply your "super" customers.

good public relations? There are many lessons all business owners can learn from this story. Here are just a few:

- Know your repeat customers' names.

- Greet each customer with eye contact and a smile.

- Create a pleasant atmosphere in your store.

- Be empathetic with your customers and their problems.

- If you can't fix a problem, let the customer know and suggest *where* they can go for a solution.

- Hire nice people, not people you have to *train* to be nice.

- Remember that word-of-mouth advertising can make or break your business.

- If your prices are higher than your competition's, let your customers know why.

- Reward your loyal customers.

- Reward your loyal employees.

Customer-retention practices have become the main survival tool of companies who are successfully riding out the current market slowdown. Focus on ways to retain and multiply your "super" customers, because they're worth it!

Conclusion

Though I don't possess a crystal ball, my experience does enable me to predict, with fairly impressive accuracy, whether a business will be successful or not. Here are the top ten points on which I base my forecasts.

A business will succeed if owners, managers, and staff...

1. ...understand that customers will always demand quality merchandise and service at a fair price.

2. ...acquire superior knowledge of their customers' wants and needs, and know how to satisfy them efficiently.

3. ...are first, last, and always, *customer focused.*

4. ...are on top of consumer behavior trends.

5. ...anticipate and react quickly to changes in customer behavior.

6. ...realize the magnitude of diversity within their customers' demographic make-up.

7. ...know that customers have more **power** and **control** than ever before and that they have unlimited information to help them make their buying decisions.

8. ...are aware that customers are intolerant of anyone who wastes their time.

9. ...understand that their customers are not just dollar signs with feet and are mindful of their feelings, wants, needs, and their right and ability to go elsewhere.

10. ...know that their customers are constantly seeking ways to balance their hectic life styles.

Understand, however, that even with the above attributes,

no business will be truly successful unless it consistently shows a deep respect for the customer, whether that customer is calling on the telephone, walking through their doors, or visiting their websites.

Respect is the key word for any business desiring to be seen as an industry leader. And no business can be considered an industry leader unless it embraces consumer differences and respects societal changes—single parent families, ethnically, racially, and culturally mixed families are shaping a new America. Baby boomers are working longer than expected and looking for ways to remain young and physically fit. Business casual is everywhere and doctors and lawyers are riding Harleys. Gen X'ers are comfortable being stay-at-home dads and corporate moms. Many are likely to have more than six careers within their life times. Home offices, multi-tasking, speed, excitement, solace and spirituality are all a part of the fabric of today's society.

Successful businesses will need to rely on customer focus groups and secret shoppers to keep their finger on the pulse of society. Those who are able to translate specific wants and needs into actual additions to their businesses will turn their customers into cheerleaders.

The time-honored principles that created successful businesses in the past will serve businesses today and in the future as long as owners and managers continue to hone, sharpen, and focus them with laser accuracy and precision.

Never forget that you must know your customer, respect your customer, and continuously seek new and creative ways to offer your product or service with value, knowledge and heart.

About the Author

Anne M. Obarski is the "Eye on Performance"

Anne Obarski is an internationally published author, professional speaker, and business consultant. For almost two decades, she has been the executive director of Merchandise Concepts, a consulting service based in Pittsburgh, Pennsylvania.

Anne works with companies that are focused on people and performance. She teaches business leaders to see their businesses through their customers' eyes. She presents keynotes and breakout sessions nationwide focusing on a business owner's two major problems: selling products or services profitably and maintaining repeat and referral customers. Her most requested topics are—

Bullfrogs Have It Easy—They Eat What Bugs Them!
How to Humanly Win People Over
Retail Business Is Show Business: *How to Razzle-Dazzle 'Em!*
Got Trust—*Wholesome Ways to Win Customers for Life*

Her company's Secret Shoppers, also known as Retail Snoops, have secretly "snooped" over two thousand stores searching for excellence in customer service. The search continues!

Anne is a contributing author of the book *Confessions of Shameless Self-Promoters* by Debbie Allen and is one of twelve experts featured in a forthcoming book, *Real World Customer Service Strategies That Really Work,* a PowerLearning book from Insight Publishing, due out in 2003.

86

She is a past president of the Pittsburgh chapter of the National Speakers Association, from which she received the Chapter Member of the Year award in 2000. She is also a professional member of the National Speakers Association and sits on the board of a number of non-profit associations.

Anne's first love is speaking to audiences about "how to reach the heart of your customers through the soul of your business." If she isn't on the speaker's platform, you just might find her on the golf course with her husband or son, or doing what truly comes naturally, shopping with her grown daughter for great bargains!

Anne M. Obarski
Merchandise Concepts
121 Kathy Ann Ct.
McMurray, PA 15317
website: *www.merchandiseconcepts.com*
e-mail: *anne@merchandiseconcepts.com*
 anne@anneobarski.com